This Place
of Wanting Nothing

poems by

Jeri Lewis Edwards

Finishing Line Press
Georgetown, Kentucky

This Place
of Wanting Nothing

Publisher: Leah Huete de Maines
Editor: Christen Kincaid
Cover Art: Jeri Lewis Edwards
Author Photo: Jeri Lewis Edwards
Cover Design: Elizabeth Maines McCleavy

Order online: www.finishinglinepress.com
also available on amazon.com

Author inquiries and mail orders:
Finishing Line Press
PO Box 1626
Georgetown, Kentucky 40324
USA

Contents

Old Faithful

I have to say something about that small improbable green of spring grass in the ebb of afternoon. The tart smell of earth from morning's rain. Crinkled foil light glinting off rippled lake. A home to darker worlds secreted in hemlock limbs. How I go there to see a glossy backed crow, the one I call Old Broken Feather with a saw-toothed wing that drags down on the right, makes him walk even more cockeyed. He inhabits this place like a room, prone to poise on the upslope, head lifted, bill opened as if he recognizes his good fortune to take flight, somehow make use of the useless. He looks at me with a sizable glance as if to acknowledge he knows for whatever is let go a taker moves right in.

I should mention this place calls me from the inside, its runted stone paths, seethe of heat in fervent sun, choir of clouds over winter gales. I am not ashamed to say I talk to Old Broken Feather when I see him, remind him old is not age related, rather an endearment. After all, I tell him while he tattoos the ground for bugs, my mother used to call me old. "Old Faithful," she'd say into the phone on my weekly calls when she still knew who I was…

I need to tell you Old Broken Feather doesn't respond, just hops about in the tall uncut near a tangle of reeds, part of the many places we leave behind. Like, where I was at the time of my mother's death: she, alone in a small room

somewhere in Maryland, and I, on the wooden walkway in front of Old Faithful (Can you believe it?) the hot plume bursting 200 feet in the icy air—
its beauty, a terrible thing.

That one time, between slumped walls in whitecap

of frozen tundra, he took me to the Old Russian settler's cabin.

Frenzied caribou whip-snapped across the plain, white

Ptarmigan unleashed from brickle reed.

His words *we have to eat* turned a language of red in my ears.

His gunmetal barrel shattered glassy air,

a caribou collapsed in silent movie shape. His marksmanship, expert

on the neck, oozed, sticky, thick . . .

a single sludge eye fixed up at us.

It smelled of our survival. I started to turn away

(this is when he told me he loved me).

His hands tucked mine inside its warm cavity,

then, like a priest raises a baptized baby from

the sepulcher, he lifted the liver

and sautéed it in a sizzle of fat.

Hope Arizona

We'd drink beer from bottles, talk
about the thirst of brown dirt,

straddle each other in the field across from the Dairy Bar,
watch moths hurl themselves against lamp posts.

How was I to know the dust and that bullet hole-ridden
milepost marker would remind me of your banality?

Outside of town a deserted jeep track undulated
like a syncopated river, where its earth ran red, and

I'd go there to lie naked in its hills, write
words you thought genius, like,

*clotted cream is cataclysmic, formidable brioche
is ruminating, patagonia cosi fan tutte . . .*

but it was to keep the days from desolation like that rupture
    of wind
that screamed off the spine of Thunder Mountain and drove one

of your horses mad—I heard you had to shoot it. Remember,
I told you the wind and your voice were the same.

Your name no longer matters

It is in this place
I am wanting nothing.

9500 feet

night glows white on pumice terrain,
the old stands of conifers emerge,
escarpment spires canopy like webs of orb spiders,
The snow melt creek is, by which I always camp,
running like hair on fire.

Some mornings I feel your presence
but I can't comprehend what you say.
It's in my imagination you're staring through
me down to the glacial lake.
That hollow where they took your eye
resembled an exhumed tree stump.
It was second nature, you once told me,
that you felt you could still see with it.
My attention begins again at a raven in flight,
say, or with a marmot scurrying across the bridal
veil precipice where I turn back to you

and you're gone.
I've lost count of the times
you've visited—you leave no trace.
Maybe, you come to interrupt the wind.
Nothing else could box with it like you could.
Sometimes traveling back down the scree
I hear the metallic scrawl
of a Clark's Nutcracker
announcing to other souls

I'm just passing through.

Landline

Standing at that payphone somewhere in Eastern Colorado, at 20, just after we eloped. The morning sun spilling colors in least expected places: rusted orange water tank, candy red fence posts, Goldfinches pecking tan dirt along the road. I didn't know what to expect when I heard my father's voice, distant through the line. I could picture him sitting on that rickety kitchen stool at the Formica counter. *Are you happy?* was all he asked. I smell the wild rye crowding at the door of the phone booth, look out on the horizon of fields, those waves of grasses, not unlike the fathomless sea of turbid white caps I left behind. Wasn't my arm holding that receiver, a wing, even then?

We're foraging for

something holy…
She always carries a .22 on her hip, so small
I only see it when she fleeces
the hardpan on her stomach as we skim
under barbed wire fences meant to keep cattle
in their grazing allotments.
Her gun accessory goes with the imperfect
language of cattle looking out of place, ranchers
with a different grasp of history on who came here
first, scarring the land
with rusted fences, rotted posts spread
like sinews over every swale.
On our off-trail ramble in this
southwestern forest, fingered washes mimic
each other, carve into the embankment
where skeletal cottonwoods slump
with atrophied limbs, gully washed roots.
The sand shifts under our weight,
my shoelaces snag on jumbled brush,
burrs ride shotgun on my boots.
Where washes cross, tracks of coyote, black-
tailed jackrabbits, Mule deer, meander with
ours—we're the interlopers.
We stoop to look at pottery
shards, turn them gently in our palms
as if they're small slumbering birds,
replace them where we found them.
In silence we
search for fox dens, cavity nesters,
brilliantly turquoise-collared lizards, discover
instead, bleached femur of calf, side
of deer jaw, hoof of javelina.

Ice Box Canyon

The truth is, you tell yourself, you're glad you've stopped pretending
that it's enjoyable to be around people. No more frivolous chatter,
gossip,

potlucks. But having confessed that, you consider that afternoon
coming out of Ice Box Canyon. Snow hard slant, white out at noon.
Three, maybe four

of us, caught in that storm, snowshoeing. We post-holed and broke
a new trail on two feet of fresh powder. No one spoke, only the fisted
crack of

snowshoe blades pushing through, lifting, planting, lifting, planting,
our breath heaving in the same rhythm. Snow weighed heavily on
firs. The sky, a dark mood

matching the slate of deep snow. Higher up, you smell aromatic
fragrance burst from crushed sagebrush. Then, a tart cry of a
Whiskey Jay warning of your intrusion.

Further ahead, a solitary buffalo, it's boulder-like backside sullen in
snow. Higher still, you look up and see the outline etch of a coyote,
sitting like a pet dog,

watching your struggle below. *Don't go,* you wanted to cry out.
But he quickly broomed through the snowbank out of sight.

It is then that you realized your heart thirsts for more of this, of each
other.

From Vevay, Dear Mom and Dad

There was nothing like this back home.
Do you remember, I'd go there once maybe twice a year
to visit Aunt Ida and Uncle Bob who married before they were out
of high school and still acted like they were young and in love
but they were older than you...and how Uncle Bob would
always carry a twinkle in his eye and call her *Aidie-Mae*
and I'd hear that special lilt in her laugh.

At ten years old, I'd sit on the stoop of their brick house
in Vevay, Indiana, staring out at the rows and rows of cornfields
and write to you, *dear mom and dad,*
today I saw three goldfinches on Aunt Ida's sunflowers
or dear mom and dad, bluebirds visited Aunt Ida's bird bath and
I found a robin's blue eggshell under the cherry tree,
and I'd wait for Uncle Bob to come home from the shoe factory
smelling of glue and leather and his hands would look like
he worked in a coal mine, and I'd ask him,
Can you take us in the back of your pick-up to the swimming hole?
and smile when he'd nod his head towards the truck
then hoist me up into the back and I'd hang on and smell the wild
honeysuckle growing alongside the road, while dust swirled around
my face and gnats clung to my shirt...There was nothing like this
back home.

Then we'd come back damp from the river and walk into Aunt Ida's
kitchen smell her fried chicken and peach pie, and I'd watch Uncle
Bob nuzzle her neck or hide a giant juicy tomato from his garden
behind his back to surprise her, but my favorite was Uncle Bob's
hushpuppies that lost count in my mouth as fireflies flashed around
us and the warm dusk breeze whispered through the corn stalks
and I'd write, *Dear mom and dad can I stay here?*

Letter From the China Rim trail

What I wanted to tell you.

When I hiked past the old corral where we used to meet, the rust of iron rose up from the ground and I felt the sweat of our bodies in the shade of those live oaks. There was a buzz of bees like the ones that swarmed above our heads, and I could hear you say, *I want your taste burned onto me.* But it was only an ache misplaced, like dreaming I have a leg and waking up to find, I don't.

I wanted to tell you my sister called. It was the day a crescendo of rain beat on the cracked earth and the wind flung a red-tailed hawk's nest to the ground outside my house. I saw the two hatchlings, still dressed in downy white feathers, clinging to a branch high in the tree, both adult hawks flying in tight circles, swooping lower and lower, as their pleading cries pierced the heavy fog.

She said the tumor behind dad's left eye had quickly grown, that the doctors didn't know if it penetrated his brain yet. I could feel her fear plunge through me, but I couldn't say what I really wanted to say, that we had arrived at the journey's arch in the bridge. Throughout the night the hawks kept crying. At dawn only one speckled hatchling was clinging to the branch.

As dusk draped the granite talus, I turned around and headed back down the trail. In the purple shadows, I heard my father's voice from far away tell me that the doctors were going to have to remove his eye to cut out the growth. I didn't recognize his tensile voice: *I wish they could do something, anything, to save my eye.* In the phone calls before his surgery, my ceaseless vigil over the hawks was something I could offer my father, the size and feathering growth of the chick, fresh kill carried by iron-like talons, those remains of squirrel and rabbit found under the tree…

As I descended the trail, in the shallow band of sunlight just ahead of me, I noticed a tarantula cross my path. I wanted to look around and tell you, but I know you're no longer there. I can still hear your voice, rich like blackberry syrup, but your face has blurred, like my streaked window, a place I keep rubbing until there is no more trace.

What I really wanted to tell you is the doctors successfully removed the tumor, but they had to take his eye. I also wanted to tell you that all three hawks flew away and didn't return.

May 11: Black Canyon

There is no saving him with his limp, the drag of a useless back leg. On the opposite bank of Blacktail Creek I watch how this thousand-pound bison pushes to distance himself from me. I imagine he knows that, save for a handful of sunrises, he'll be sustenance for grizzly or wolf. . . perhaps the lone wolf trotting off on the plateau above, or the unseen members of his pack probably watching me. But I don't feel a need to save him, airlift him out of this mud to a society of plastic pools and fast food. I adjust my pack and carry on to where a bald eagle above banks into view, maybe or maybe not the same one I've seen all along this section of trail.

With the tumble of the Yellowstone far below, dips and swales of every bend, I discover chalky white bones, scattered like dreams of my youth. My destination: a backcountry camp on a broad strand of the Yellowstone River. Along the high-ridged trail, I witness vestiges of winter's war: bloated bison contorted between mammoth boulders, elk hides, long pulled from their skeletons, and a cavity of rancid meat. Could I, would I if I were starving, carve from it? After ten miles, my camp is full of river song in my ears. Light snow dusts the tarp I huddle beneath.

I think of that injured magnificent beast adorned with a massive shoulder hump and shagged wooly mane. I say to the earth, let him lay down his head where shooting stars erupt from snow-edged meadows—or if he can make it that far, south along the banks of Hellroaring Creek.

Before dark encloses my tent, before hail staccatos my sleep, I kneel beside a perfect print of a mountain lion on the sandy bar. At dawn, every trace vanished in the rain-soaked slope.

I look down in a pocket of shallow current.
A thigh bone of a small deer shifts in the ripple.

When It Rained

I.

When I ran, it rained.
It was in mid-autumn, the dense forest
became shrouded in translucent hues of cinnamon and rum, a fine
mist twisted around knurled trunks and milky quartz, the sluice of
mud and leaves oozed beneath my feet. I had been thinking of him,
his skin, smooth like Manzanita bark. My fingers, red-tipped and
raw, ached for his warmth. His gasp barely audible, "*hold me there.*"

When I ran, it rained harder.
Near a swath of moss I reached for a small
wintergreen leaf, tore its soft green flesh to release its aroma. As the
rain dripped down my back, he whispered into my mouth, I wanted
to swallow his words under water.

II.

When I biked, the rain stung my eyes.
The rolling countryside became late autumn, redolent of pregnant
vineyards, of the air's fragrance of grapes, the distant tinkling
of sheep's bells down the hills. "*Meet me in Lucca,*" his voice traveled
through the static phone lines. "*I'll ride mia bicicletta,*" I replied.

En route from Firenze, the asphalt-colored sky opened up, incessant
traffic, fumes, waterlogged roads, all poured through me. Soaked
and mud-streaked, I arrived at the small *pensione* . . . I thought about
his dark eyes, how I could swim in them. "*Brutta tempo,*" I shivered,
dripping a puddle on the doorstep. His strong arms pulled me
into his chest, wrapped a towel around me. He offered me a cup of
espresso. *E appena arrivata,* he had been waiting for me. On an
entryway table, wildflowers overflowed in a vase, the same ones that
had blanketed the sides of the road, their profuse blossoms
turned electric blue in the rain.

Focus on that incandescent sky

directly above your head. Now, try to hold your chin up high, thrust your head back while holding your eyes half-shut. That was my niece, barely having the muscle to tilt her head back when she sat in that wheelchair down at the old oak, under the flare of shade. There'd appear a brief interval of smile when she'd see the light dappling down like spare change through the catacombs of limbs, restless leaves drowning out voices in front of her, voices behind, whispering, always whispering, "poor girl."

She spent her formative years upright on her knees, getting around the house, up and down the carpeted stairs, the linoleum basement, the oil-stained garage, developing driftwood-sized calluses before her mother acknowledged
   the necessity of a wheelchair.

But I'm not telling you this for the sake of pity. What I really want you to imagine is how she'd sit in that wheelchair, head held back, those eyes half open, lifting her arms like twigs, flailing her puny unused hands to try to reach those leaves, the tree's crags and crotches, those snags and fractals. For anything, everything.

You Always Had the Sea Bass

You didn't smoke, yet

you'd pocket the glossy black matchbox
and clear your throat from time to time
as if you might say something,
but never did.
You'd wear your usual café stare as
we'd watch the drudge of commuters,
read the menu we knew by heart, sift through
topics haphazardly:
water main break on Columbus,
glacial meltdown in Antarctica,
reported sightings of a Snowy Owl in Central Park,
and in the iridescent candlelight,
the fluid smiles of other diners glimmered
the way the moon ripples on the Hudson.
It's been years since our Upper Westside
neighborhood, but I still have some of those
shiny matchboxes you collected.
Turned in the palm of my hand, I can almost
see your finger smudge.
Like an old photograph,
I try to search for more, somewhere along
the coast of Big Sur, hunkered down
in front of a roaring fire in July,
but I can't remember what we talked about,

how we filled the air.

You Might Not Know

I can't tell you the exact time,
but it was when I walked
along that old orchard trail, I realized
that you are not
the delectable apricot found
ripe on the tree.
And it hurts to tell you
that you can never be
the juice of the melon
that dribbles down my chin.

I forgot to tell you,
you were once the swells
that crash ashore,
the gait of sandpipers that skirt
the sea foam, the moon's watery
glow on our lips.

I thought you could be the impasto
gleam of sun against the distant sandstone
peak, but I know now that I can never
make you close to being
the prismatic vapor trails
illuminated across the striated skies,
the ones that made us gasp,
or was it that we were so new
in love. And just before I discarded that
tattered photo album, it became clear
to me that you were never the stuffing in
Helen Mae's turkey, or the wild mushroom
soup at Gramercy Tavern
on those rain-soaked nights in the city.

You once told me
I was the western wind
in your sails, but I was desperate to be
the wild mustard blowing unbridled
along a coastal hillside,
even the heady fragrance of an aged
Chateauneuf du Pape would have sufficed.

But don't worry, you won't be hearing me
in the thunder in a nearing storm, or
the lightning reflected across
the chrome on your bumper.

No matter what,
you'll always be those high-tide swells,
the ones in my youth,
when I summered at the Cape.
Isn't that enough?

High Tide

His screams,
the kind you can't shut out,
the kind that sounds of death
when our neighbor ran over
his dog in the driveway...
the look on my brother's face,
his poached-egg eyes,
wider than when we'd dared
each other to ride
the scariest rides
down at the county fair
on those humid August nights.
Dad was dragging him
through the sand, holding him tight,
his muscles bulged in the white
space above his farmer's tan,
his teeth clamped down on his tongue,
I thought he'd bite right through it.
Brother's short legs
flailed to kick Dad's shins,
"No, no, don't make me."
Dad's voice arced with the crash
of the waves, *"No son of mine*
is going to be scared of the ocean."
I tried to run fast
but my feet sank with each thrust,
back to the beach house,
up the stairs to the wooden deck,
out of breath, pushing
the tattered screen aside. I saw
Mom over the stove, a fork
that moved slowly in her hands.
The smell of bacon filled the room.

"Did you wipe the sand off your feet?"
I cried, *"Dad is trying to drown him."*
She didn't turn to look at me.
I could see the apron tied
neatly around her waist.
I could hear the grease pop.

Speaking in Tongues

It's something like 97 degrees in the shade
when you start out at the trailhead.
Late afternoon rays caramelize the muscled mountains.

Heat, wrapped in wind,
carries no refuge up the switchbacked path . . .
the cup of your back a hollow of sweat
doesn't deter from what's ahead.

The relentless rise abrupts a series of swales,
a pulpy chaparral, another short burst,
a scramble over pockmarked boulders,
then a wide yielding turn where color
ignites color—solitude meets the sky.

At the three-fingered wash,
you note all springs have run dry, there's
no succor in this season.

A Wrentit's staccato in a stand of valley oaks
entices you to linger,
but you persevere to crest before sundown.

And somewhere along this path,
in an inexplicable moment,
expansiveness of this space
takes you out of your place,
recalibrates your inner plumb line.

And though you arrive at the summit,
feet heavy, mouth chalky,
an internal renewal resonates.

Raptors rush overhead, swoop for kill
down the folds of ravines,
quail scribble in crumbled leaves,
lizards scurry like sandpaper in parched grass.

The last paean of light drapes silk on distant crags—
you stand motionless, but not alone.
Wildness speaks in tongues to those who listen.

Acrostic Sky Writing

Juxtaposed against the landscape, barren and dry,
Emergent on my tongue, the morning coolness mixed with
Rivers of heat wafting up on that
Island, a sky island, just

Like when we were in the Chiracahuas,
Even in the Santa Ritas,
With the silvery-veined hares evanescent as the dew on the

cholla,

I remember only how we got there,
Suddenly looking into a deep ravine where,

Encased, the finality of us echoed off the canyon called
Dante's Wall, the sunrise at your back.
When you cleared your throat again, (I thought you had coughed,)
And raised your voice, for out there, who would
Repeat it, that after all those years, you emphasized 'all',
Didn't I read your journal in secret, didn't I
See this coming?

None of this is ours to hold onto

An unusually cold or gray day—even
rainy Sundays are best. A language specific to us on our walks in the
woods,

> just me and my dogs.

8 am, the forest brims with a deluge of want.
Strange sounds emanate from misshapen trees, limbs become broken
fingers, leaves, immaculate tongues, chipped
bark, lost teeth. Birds and other animals are hunkered down,

> just me and my dogs.

The dogs run in circles, zigging in front,
zagging behind, whisking straight up the track and in reverse, quickly
taking on a feral appearance, happily
matted with shards of paper birch, pine needles, indescribably
orange fungi that hang like ornaments off flanks and ribs.

Down and up and around the twists we go, aiming towards
anything, spending all day out there when we can,
sometimes dripping in mud and sand, sometimes
returning to the vehicle with only a pencil
stub of light in the winter sky, looking to begin
all of this again tomorrow.

It's the taller one,
only six years old, her white fur
pulverized by rain, muck, sweat. She holds her gaze on me,
dense like the understory, layers of devotion.
She lingers longer now, pushes herself to keep up.

> How do I dispel my craving for what isn't?

Again and again the agony that cancer is taking her.

Taking. Her.

Nothing is next

except the night comes.

Bedded down we become a family of deer,
our red blanket, a pocked depression,
        a sweet artifice suspended.

Even when she's gone, I know
I'll lean over to where her warm body
completed the space, and whisper,

        it was good, wasn't it?

The Gift Between Us

Her black shape appears at first light,
perched in a snag near my bedroom window,
crack of sun not yet breaking over the hills.
She's murmuring a few of her Raven *quarks, kruks,*
prodding, waiting for me. I've noticed this spring
she's got five chicks in a nest to feed, so, I'm out
the door every morning with suet. I try not to make too much
of it, this sharing, her acknowledgment.
It's a quiet privilege to witness her secretive routine
nuanced under one folded wing.
There's no intent to consider her a pet—no giving her a name—
rather, I consider the fat I offer to her an homage
to her fated toil in this high desert scrab.
Placed discreetly on a distant boulder,
she and her mate voraciously stuff their bills,
whoosh back to their nest in the highest Juniper,
and quiet their chicks' frenetic mouths.
For this, on a pre-dawn morning, she places,
side by side on my doorstep,
as if they were a calligrapher's quill and ink,
one of her primary feathers and a twig.

(Photo by Jeri Lewis Edwards of the raven's gift exactly as found)

Refugium

I am not
the confluence of spine, the flush-flash-
bash of a river's untethered soul,
the Verde, venerate falls in the Firehole, or fill of air
in lost smells...I am not
the Watersmeet, the place where our lips met,
those inconsequential discoveries. . .not
the Rappahannock, the rivulet not yet formed
in miscarriage, Bagaduce, Housatonic,
the cataract of rapids to your heart,
the crutch in the Snake, or the sinuous meanders from
the Columbia, the cliff
house set on a failed marriage,
where what we found by water's edge vanished
outside of dreams . . .
not the oxbow's abandoned loop of river channel
no longer recognizable in the wildness of our past,
or the Neversink, the receding San Pedro, nor
the surge of sea to the imperturbable estuary—
Instead, I'll be that vast migration, that
long-distance warbler, the Chiricahua Sky Island
where they'll carry my body in a burlap bag
to the 9,000-foot crest, lie me on sprigs
of Winterfat, fragrant Algerita, and leave me at last,
to the eternal song of the Hermit Thrush.

ACKNOWLEDGMENTS

I thank the editors of the following journals for first publishing these poems, some of them with different titles and in slightly different forms:

Confluence: "You might not know" and "From Vevay, Dear Mom and Dad"

Dulcet Literary Magazine: "None of this is ours to hold onto"— nominated for Pushcart Prize

Green Ink Poetry: "We're foraging for"

Long River Review: "Focus on that incandescent sky"

Lullwater: "You Always Had the Sea Bass"

Naugatuck River Review: "Old Faithful" formerly, "The Many Places We Leave Behind"

Phantasmagoria: "Acrostic Sky Island"

Poet Lore: "When it Rained"

The Portland Review: "Speaking in Tongues"

Prairie Winds: "High Tide"

Rivendell: "What I wanted to tell you from China Rim"

The Stillwater Review: "The Gift Between Us"

Talking Writing: "May 11: Black Canyon," formerly, "Scattered Bones"

The Writer's Journal: "Ice Box Canyon"

Wee Sparrow Poetry Press Anthology: "Refugium"

Westwind Review: "Hope Arizona"

Wild Roof Journal: "Your Name No Longer Matters"

The Worcester Review: "That one time between slumped walls in whitecaps"

Jeri Lewis Edwards is a mixed media artist, poet, and naturalist residing along the Central Coast of California. Nominated for a Pushcart Prize, her poems and visual art have been published in numerous literary journals such as *Dulcet Literary Magazine, Silver Birch Press, Poet Lore, Naugatuck River Review, The Penn Review, The Stillwater Review, Cool Beans Lit, Long River Review, The Wee Sparrow Poetry Press, Green Ink Poetry, Wild Roof Journal*, among many others. Every day you'll find her out walking or hiking with her rescue dogs, and in her art studio, 2Ravens Studio, endeavoring each day to learn something from nature and from her art. You can find some of her work on Instagram: *@Jeri2ravensstudio.*